# Mommy
## to the Office

## Gulden Mesara-Dogan

ISBN-10: 149231417X
ISBN-13: 9781492314172

Library of Congress Control Number: 2013916195
LCCN Imprint Name: City and State (If applicable)

This story is for Selin and Sarper

*When I go to school in the morning, my mommy goes to work.*

My mommy, daddy and brother eat breakfast with me every morning. I love toast with strawberry jam. My mommy likes cereal and milk.

After breakfast, my mommy gets ready for work. She chooses the clothes she wants to wear. Then she brushes her hair and puts on her makeup.

*She puts her notebook,*

*cell phone, and computer*

*in her bag.*

*As I walk to the bus stop to go to school, my mommy leaves for work.*

My mommy works in a big building. Lots of other people work there, too.

In her office, my mommy has a big desk. She also has a telephone, a cup of pens, and lots of pictures of me and my brother.

My mommy misses me when she is at work, just like I sometimes miss her when I'm at school. When she misses me, she looks at my photos. They make her happy.

My mommy's day is
very busy. She talks on the
telephone, sends e-mails from
her computer, and has lots
of meetings.

When she is hungry,
she eats lunch. Sometimes she
eats at the office's cafeteria.
Sometimes she goes to lunch
with friends or packs a lunch
and eats it at her desk.

When I am big, I will go to work like my mommy does. My mommy says I have to go to school first, though.

*At the end of the day, my mommy comes back home. She gives me a big hug and a kiss.*

"I missed you so much,"
says my mommy.
"I missed you too, Mommy,"
I tell her.

In the evening, we eat dinner together. I help set the table. My mommy calls me her "little helper."

*After dinner, we play*

*with my toys.*

When it's time for bed, my mommy helps me get ready. We brush our teeth together. She picks out my pajamas.

My mommy reads two stories before bed. I pick one story and my brother picks another one. "Now it's time to sleep," she says after finishing the last one. "Good night, sleepyhead. I love you." I know that the next day, we'll do it all again.